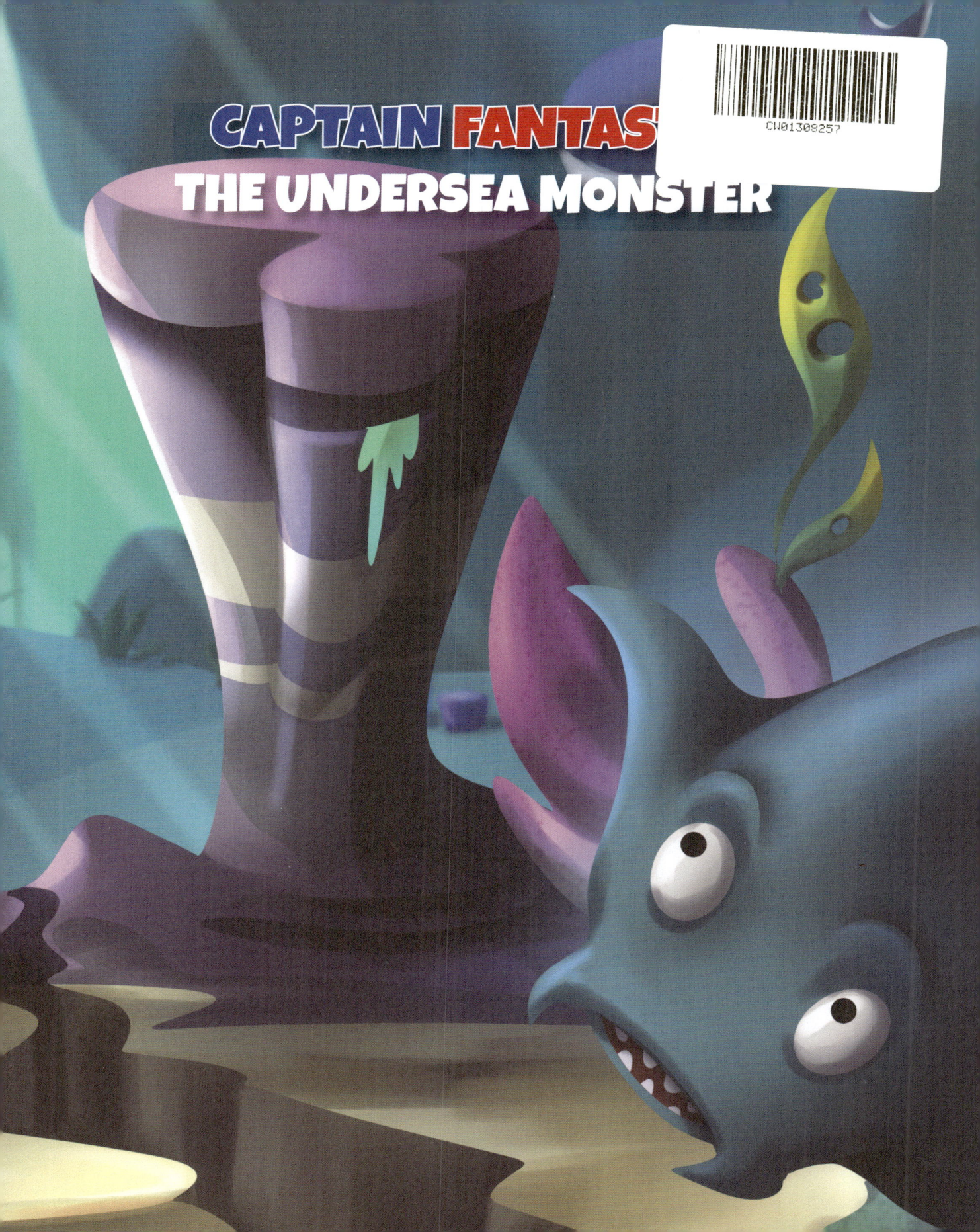

THIS BOOK BELONGS TO

....

THE CAPTAIN FANTASTIC COLLECTION

Published by Tommy Balaam, founder of Captain Fantastic
UK's No.1 children's entertainment company
www.captain-fantastic.co.uk

Copyright © 2024 Tommy Balaam
Cover and illustrations by Daniel Howard, xxdanielhowardxx@gmail.com
Book design by Helen Nelson, www.jetthedog.co.uk
Editing by Ilsa Hawtin, www.wordsure.co.uk

All rights reserved. No part of this book may be used or reproduced without written permission from the author, except in the case of brief quotations in critical articles or review.
ISBN: 9798879595789

CAPTAIN FANTASTIC

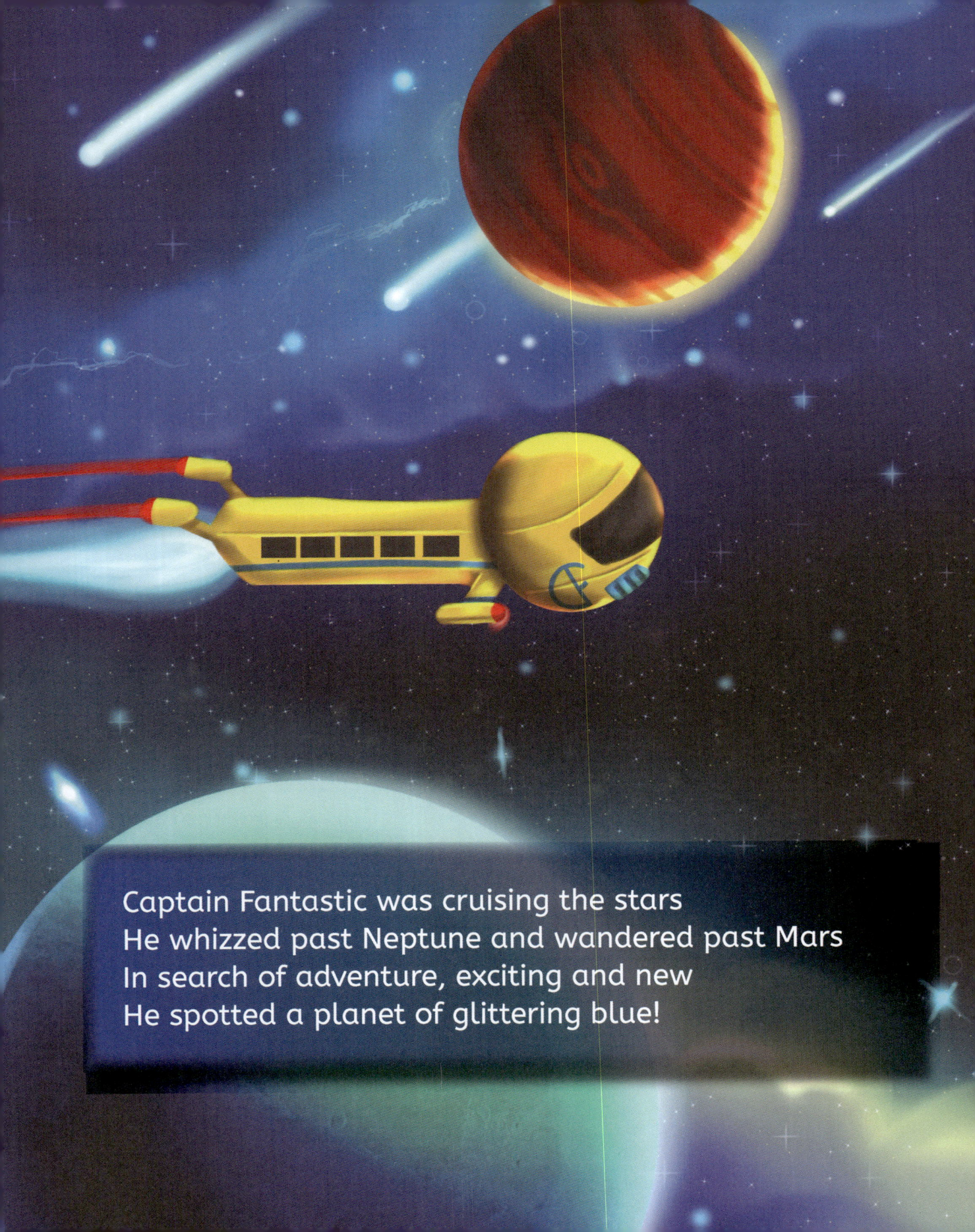

Captain Fantastic was cruising the stars
He whizzed past Neptune and wandered past Mars
In search of adventure, exciting and new
He spotted a planet of glittering blue!

"An ocean!" he cried, as he peeped through his scope
"Fantastic," he said, "let's visit! I hope
There'll be nurtles and mantas and tickle kelp too,
Gigglefish, starminnows and plenty to do."

The Captain and Winston splashed down in their ship
Captain popped on his goggles and started to slip
Into his wetsuit and snorkel and fins
But Winston the space dog refused to jump in!

"No, thank you," he said. "I'd rather stay dry
I'll read a good book, and maybe I'll try
To catch us fish dinner with my shiny new rod
Some tuna or haddock or mackerel or cod."

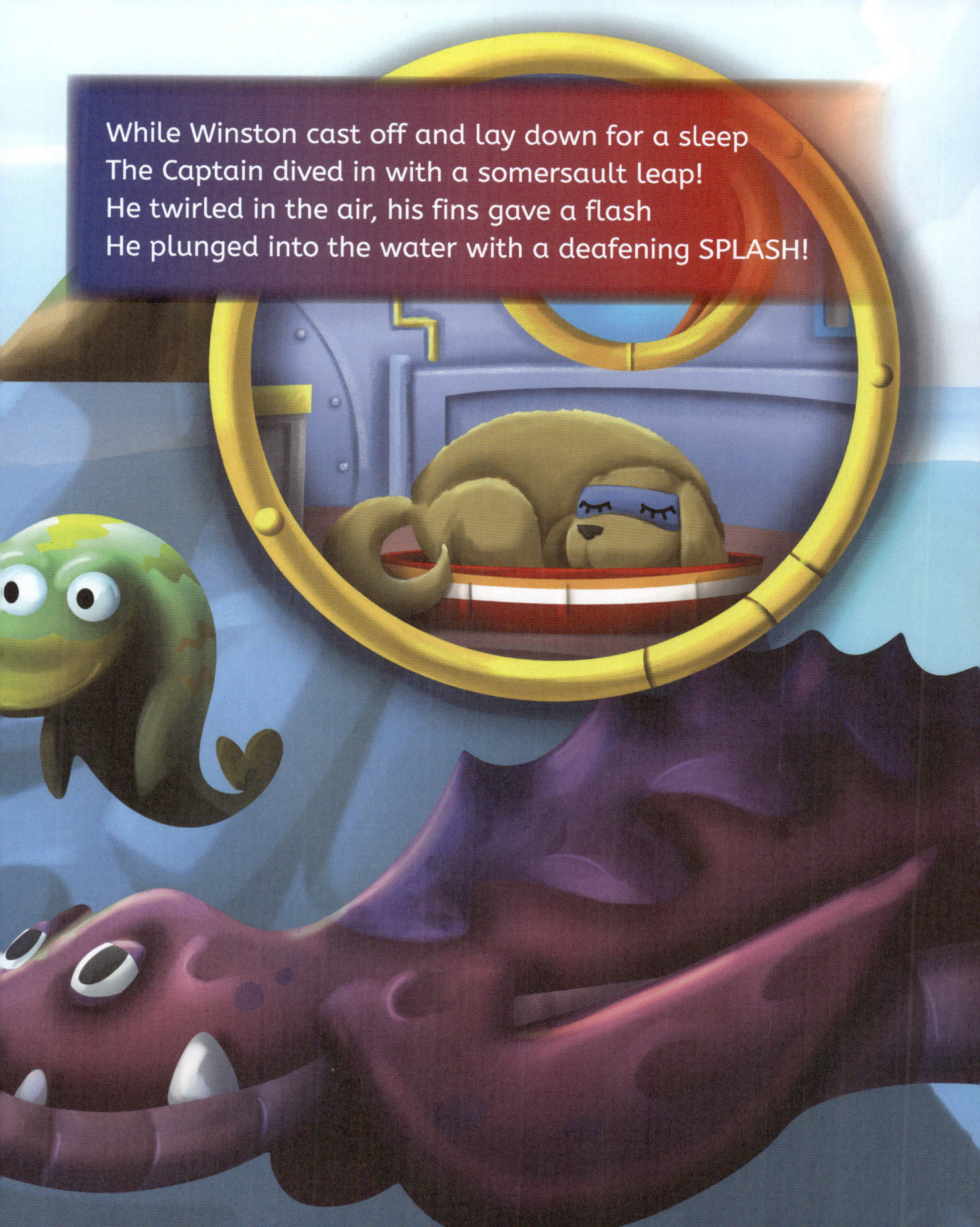

While Winston cast off and lay down for a sleep
The Captain dived in with a somersault leap!
He twirled in the air, his fins gave a flash
He plunged into the water with a deafening SPLASH!

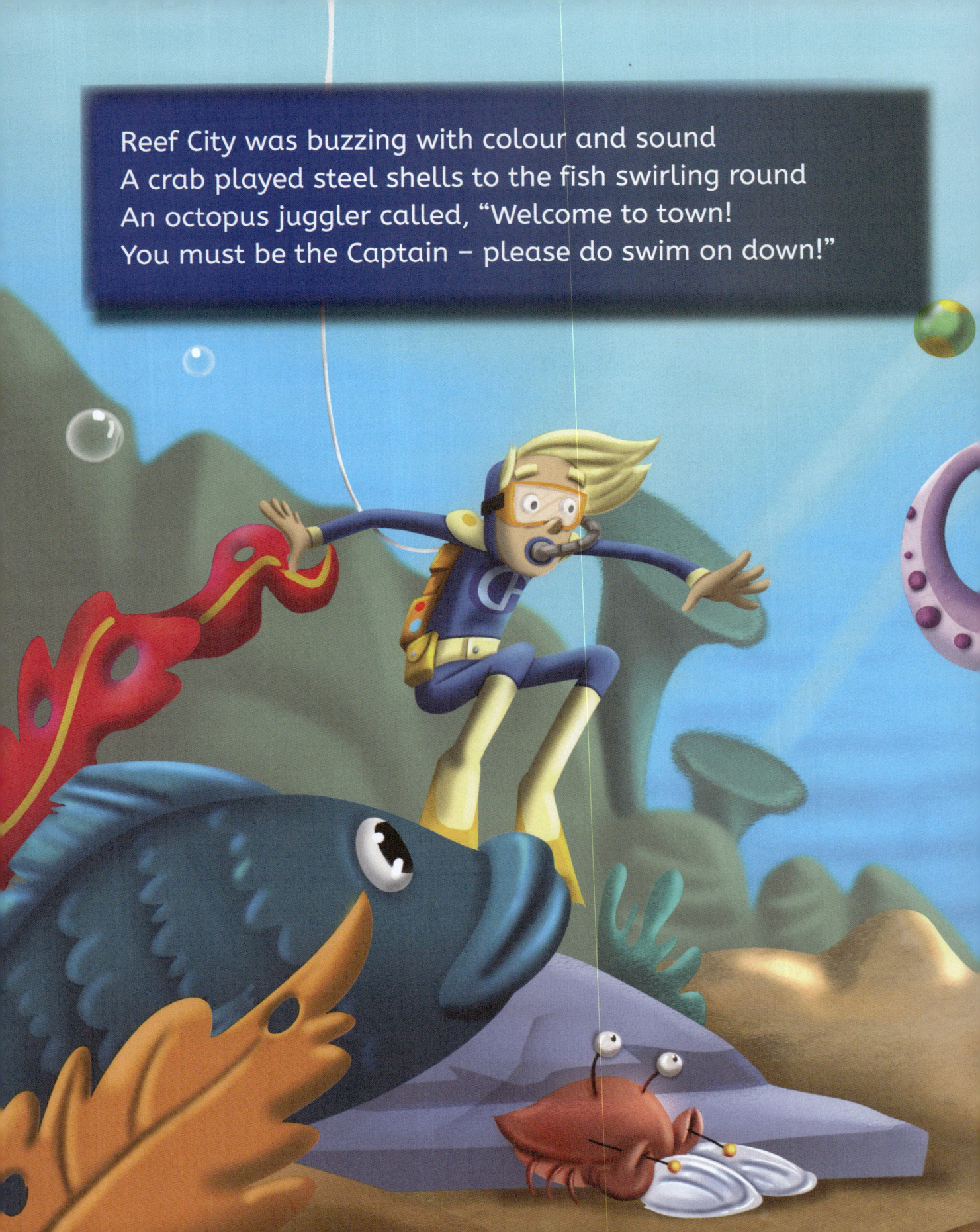

Reef City was buzzing with colour and sound
A crab played steel shells to the fish swirling round
An octopus juggler called, "Welcome to town!
You must be the Captain – please do swim on down!"

A pufferfish boomed, "If you're here for a visit
The Space Seahorse Circus is simply exquisite
Though if you swim further, I should let you know
It's not safe for visitors deep down below."

But Captain Fantastic was keen to explore
Reef City was lively, but he wanted more!
As he swam deeper, the water grew colder
With jaggedy rocks and raggedy boulders.

A dazzling disco of nightlife shone bright
Eels and lantern fish spotted with lights
Jellyfish jived and strobed in the dark
And guarding the door was an enormous shark.

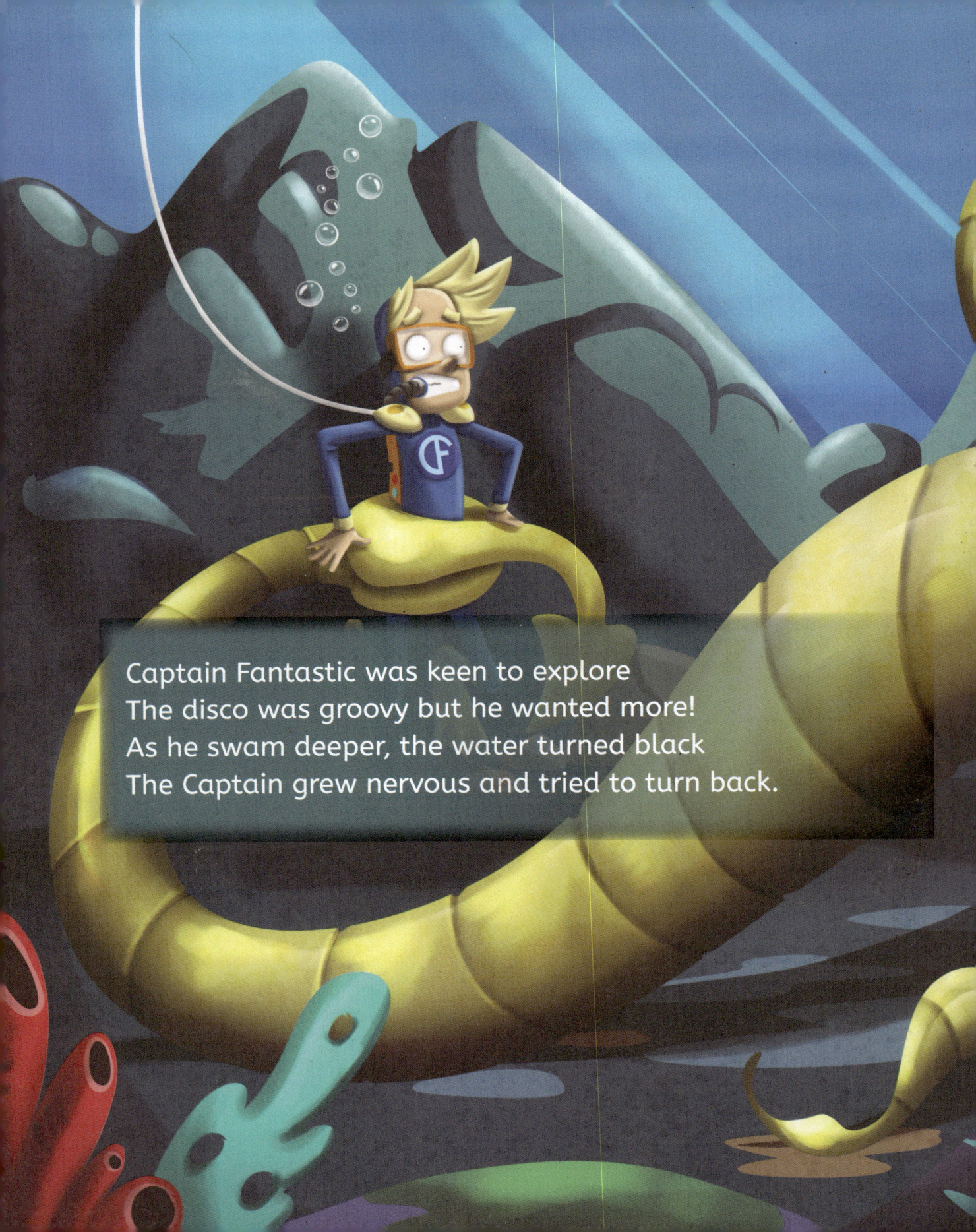

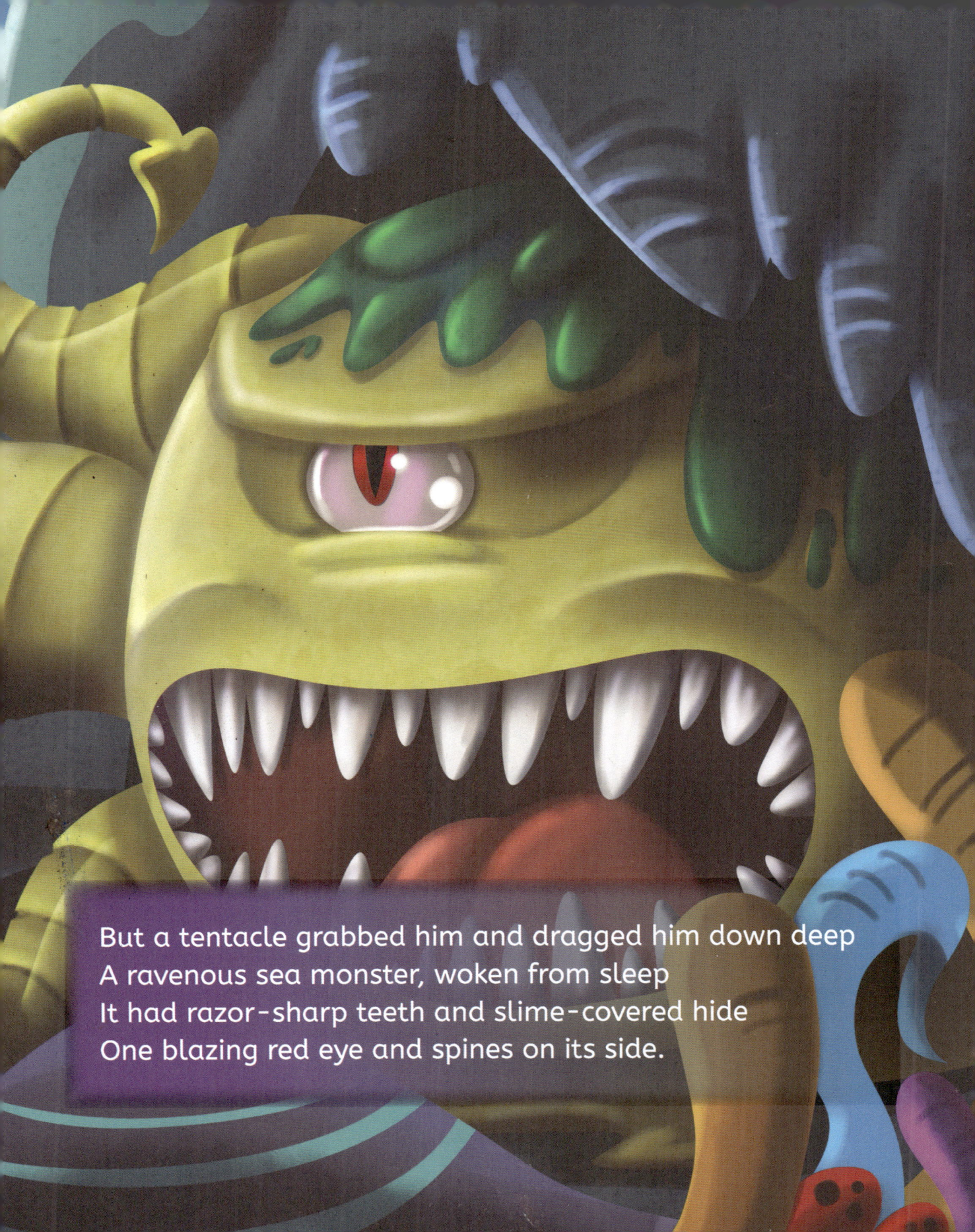

But a tentacle grabbed him and dragged him down deep
A ravenous sea monster, woken from sleep
It had razor-sharp teeth and slime-covered hide
One blazing red eye and spines on its side.

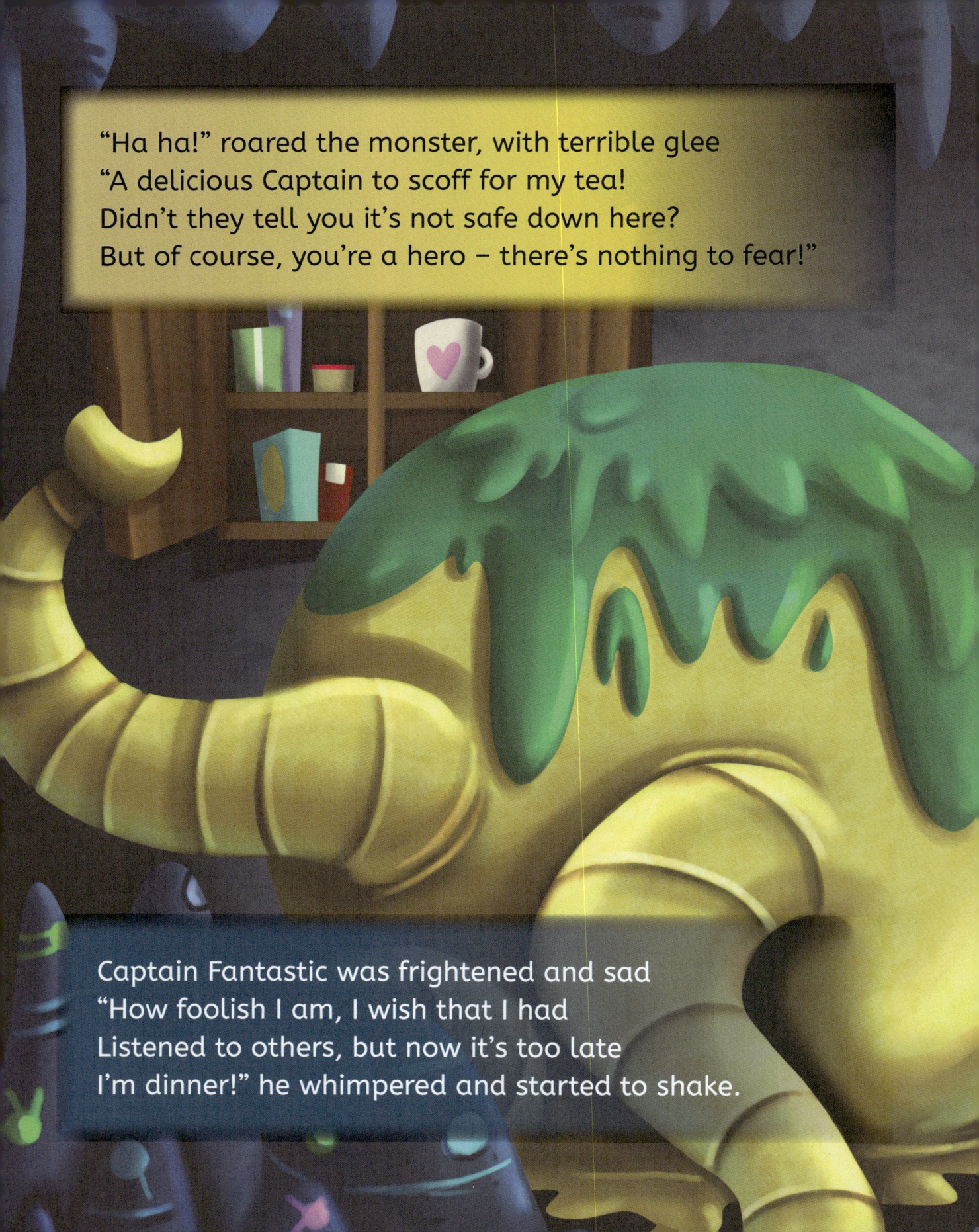

"Ha ha!" roared the monster, with terrible glee
"A delicious Captain to scoff for my tea!
Didn't they tell you it's not safe down here?
But of course, you're a hero – there's nothing to fear!"

Captain Fantastic was frightened and sad
"How foolish I am, I wish that I had
Listened to others, but now it's too late
I'm dinner!" he whimpered and started to shake.

High up above, Winston's line gave a quiver
He felt the vibrations of the poor Captain's shiver
"The Captain afraid? Now, that can't be good."
And he reeled in his line as quick as he could.

The sea monster drooled and licked its foul lips
When suddenly the Captain shot from its grip!
Like a cork from a bottle, he whizzed through the dark
Zoomed past the eels and startled the shark.

With a grunt, Winston scooped him onboard with a paw
"Thanks," said the Captain. "Without you, I'm sure
I would have been sea monster supper instead!"
He felt foolish and small as he hung his head.

"Don't worry," said Winston. "Just next time be sure
To listen to others before you explore."
He made him hot cocoa and tucked him up tight
"Sweet dreams," Winston said, "sleep well and goodnight."

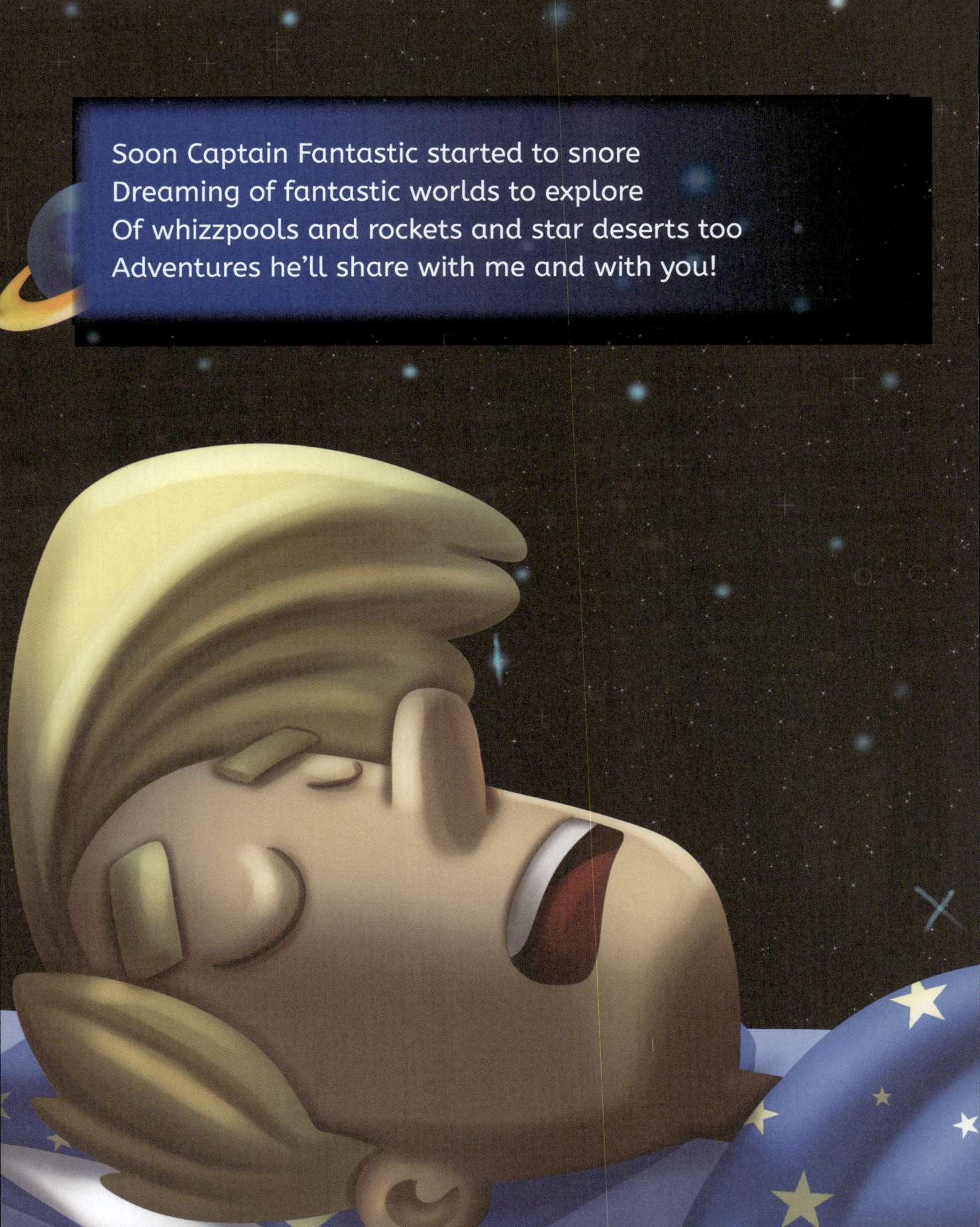

Soon Captain Fantastic started to snore
Dreaming of fantastic worlds to explore
Of whizzpools and rockets and star deserts too
Adventures he'll share with me and with you!

CAPTAIN FANTASTIC

VOTED THE UK'S NUMBER ONE CHILDREN'S ENTERTAINMENT COMPANY

COME AND JOIN US!

Welcome to Captain Fantastic, your go-to destination for award-winning children's party entertainment. We've proudly earned the title of the 'UK's Number One Children's Entertainment Company,' as recognized by FreeIndex, 'What's on for Kids,' and Junior Magazine. We are the go-to choice for families across the UK and now in the USA!

Beyond our incredble parties, why not explore our Amazon bestselling kids' books, where our beloved characters come to life.

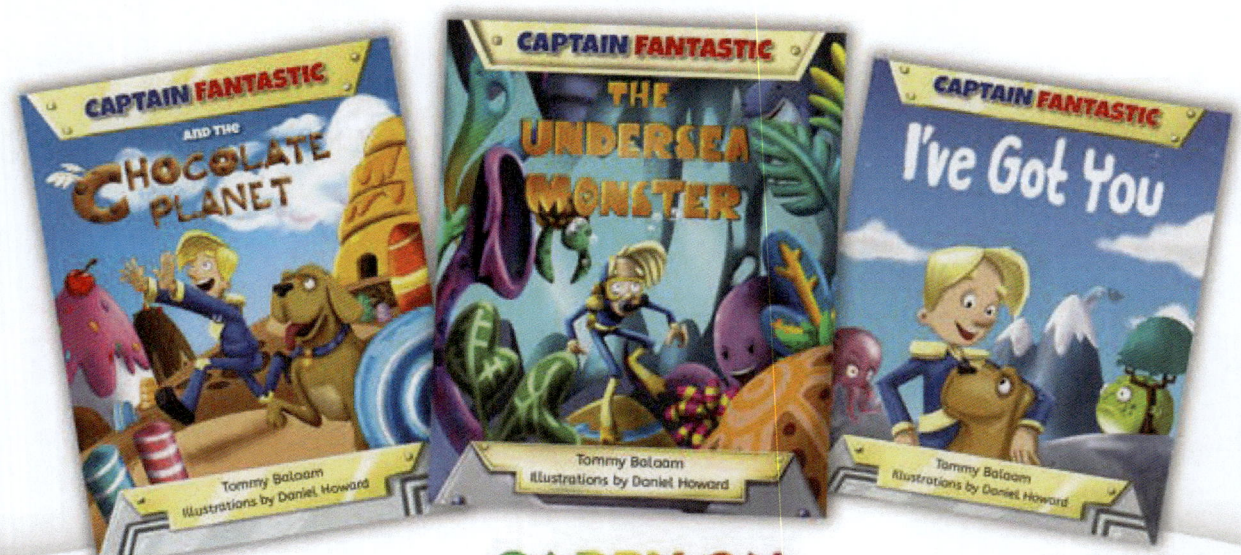

CARRY ON THE ADVENTURE

Discover the exciting world of Captain Fantastic on YouTube! Join in the fun by searching for 'Captain Fantastic Adventures' or scan the QR code.

SCAN ME!

WWW.CAPTAIN-FANTASTIC.CO.UK

Printed in Great Britain
by Amazon